EAST OF LEICESTER

The church of St Catherine, Houghton-on-the-Hill, 1793.

Lowesby station, 1950. Standing on the platform, left to right, are Mr J. Spark, Alf Baines and the station-master, Fred Lant. Like so many small stations in high Leicestershire, this was a jewel in the landscape. It was superbly maintained, and the station-master, porter and railway workers took pride in their place of employment. They kept the track and station clean and tidy, painting the woodwork and above all planting and maintaining superb gardens, often at their own expense. Competitions were run for the best-kept station. It was an honour to be awarded the prize for the finest in the region.

BRITAIN IN OLD PHOTOGRAPHS

EAST OF LEICESTER

TREVOR HICKMAN

SUTTON PUBLISHING LIMITED

Sutton Publishing Limited
Phoenix Mill · Far Thrupp · Stroud
Gloucestershire · GL5 2BU

First published 1996

Cover photographs: Front: Queniborough,
1904. Back: Houghton-on-the-Hill, *c.* 1940.
Title page: Barkby church font, 1791.

By the same author:
Around Melton Mowbray in Old Photographs
Melton Mowbray in Old Photographs
The Vale of Belvoir in Old Photographs
The History of Stilton Cheese
Around Rutland in Old Photographs

British Library Cataloguing in Publication Data
A catalogue record for this book is available from the
British Library.

ISBN 0-7509-1428-9

Typeset in 10/12 Perpetua.
Typesetting and origination by
Alan Sutton Publishing Limited.
Printed in Great Britain by
Ebenezer Baylis, Worcester.

The church of All Saints, Lowesby, 1793.

CONTENTS

The junction of the Scraptoft to Keyham roads, April 1951.

INTRODUCTION

For many years I have had an interest in the area of countryside to the east of Leicester. Living in a village on the extreme eastern edge of the county, I normally travel by car into the city along minor roads through some fine countryside and delightful villages. This book is made up from a personal selection, placing on record much of what I consider was and is the best of rural England. I have included photographs of people wherever possible. The book also gives a small indication of what has been lost through urban development, which I consider began with land enclosure and was given considerable impetus through the influence of eighteenth-century industrial expansion. Consolidated with the economic growth of the country during the Victorian period, that has continued to the present day.

Leicester (*Ratae* to the Romans, who built a town on a previous occupation site) laid out a system of roads between the years AD 100 and 150. Some are still with us today. The Fosse Way runs through Leicester, a Roman road that travels down the spine of England, passing through Thurmaston and Syston. About the year AD 120 a milestone was erected on the Fosse Way two miles to the north of *Ratae*; this stone still survives. Evidence of the Roman occupation is on display in the Jewry Wall museum, and many Romano-British sites have been located in and around villages to the east of Leicester. The Romans had departed by the year AD 410. The area eventually came under the control of the Saxons and the Danes.

The area covered in this book is noted for its deserted villages and hamlets. Some would have been built by Saxon farmers, such as the small settlements at Quenby and Ingarsby. The latter deserted hamlet appears to be of Danish origin. 'Ingwar' was a Danish family name, hence Ingars village. 'By' was a Swedish/Danish word denoting farm or farmstead, not a village but a hamlet, hence 'Ingars-by'. There are six deserted villages and hamlets of considerable archaeological importance lying in the fields only a short distance from the city of Leicester. The reason for their demise is not easily explained, but undoubtedly the Black Death that first visited the area in 1349 played its part. In my opinion blame should be placed on the landowners, who considered they needed the land for personal gain. The plague visited most villages in the Midlands; very few did not recover. Unscrupulous landlords were motivated to clear the villages through a change in agricultural policy. The open field system of cultivation was labour intensive; enclosing the fields into larger units for sheep and cattle grazing meant that only a few farm workers were required to maintain the herds. These people worked for the landlord as his tenants. Fleece, milk (cheese, etc.), hides and meat showed a higher return in relation to the tithe extracted from the villagers working their strips of arable land scattered around the village.

The large estates that developed as a result of the clearance programme still exist, in part, in the area covered in this book. Of these Quenby is the most prominent. The Ashbys owned land throughout the area from the late twelfth century onwards and were responsible for an enclosure clearance programme involving areas far greater than the present estate. They built a manor house at Quenby and on this site, between the years 1615 and 1620, George Ashby constructed the present hall, a magnificent brick building that dominates the landscape.

With the enclosing of the open fields farming methods changed. The enclosing acts of the 1760s completed the process. In these pages I have included many photographs of farming activities and of course photographs of fox-hunters. Today it is a controversial sport, seen by many people as cruel and unnecessary. It must be realized that like so many country pursuits it developed through necessity. With the enclosing of the fields and the simultaneous digging of ditches and planting of hedges, a ready-made series of concealed tracks with cover was provided for the cunning fox. The animal flourished and thrived on food such as young lambs and of course rabbits from the warrens that were also maintained to provide a constant supply of meat. The simplest way to kill a fox is to run it down with dogs bred for the purpose. The same process of control had happened with the wolf; a less resilient animal, it was exterminated. The fox population was controlled by determined farmers, and considerable bounty was paid for each brush (tail), often by the village constable! This all changed in the late eighteenth century as landowners had more leisure time. They were no longer involved in preparing for mounted cavalry charges in continuous national and continental wars.

A heron fishing in the nature reserve, Watermead Country Park, Thurmaston. This development came out of 1950s clay and gravel extraction. The heronry is a feature of this reserve; these birds can be viewed from a purpose-built hide constructed by the Leicestershire County Council.

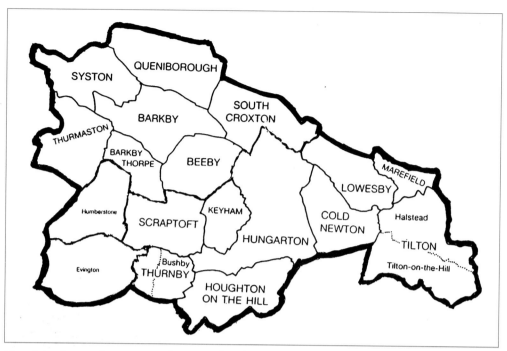

Plan of the nineteenth-century parishes covered in this publication.

Hunting on horseback, following a pack of hounds, became a source of pleasure. The thrill of the chase, jumping the hedges and fences of the enclosed fields after an elusive fox now became a sport, not a means of keeping down a vicious pest. The fox population increased, helped by the planting of fox coverts. Such small groups of trees are scattered across the landscape to the east of Leicester.

The growth of the city of Leicester is very apparent when one examines the sections of the 1867 edition of the Ordnance Survey that I have included in the book. It is a city of considerable industrial importance; the first canal arrived in 1796 when the River Soar running into the River Trent was canalized. The first train left Leicester in 1832, and in the pages of this book I have included a number of nostalgic photographs of railway stations and steam trains. The Victorians expanded Leicester, and some of this expansion can be seen in the photographs I have selected. In 1885 Spinney Hill Park was laid out to a design by Cecil Ogden. On the 1867 map printed on page 9 the area is still shown as open fields. Mineral extraction too has played its part in shaping the landscape. Iron ore from the Halstead pit and the removal of clay and gravel from the Soar valley has resulted in the construction of Watermead Countryside Park, with the splendid nature reserve on the west side of Thurmaston.

I trust readers of this book will find this collection of interest and will enjoy it in the spirit that it is presented, as a record of a beautiful and interesting area of England.

LEICESTER

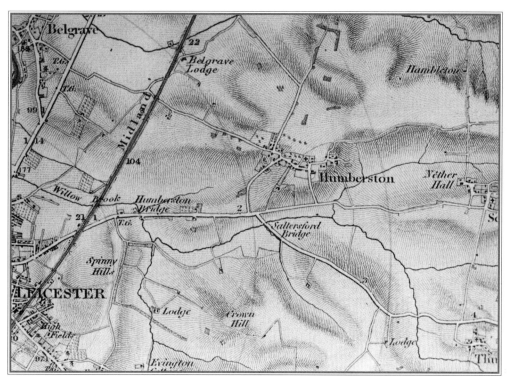

A section of the Ordnance Survey map engraved by B. & A. Baker and published on 20 June 1835 by Lt-Col. Colby of the Royal Engineers. It was revised in 1867. In the period 1835 to 1867 the east of Leicester was still a rural area; note Spinny Hills, Highfields and the open area of countryside between the city and the small village of Humberstone.

EVINGTON

Church Road, 1904. The cottage on the right has been demolished; the modern house on the site is Barn House no. 77.

The church of St Denys viewed from across open fields (now the church car park) in 1904. The vicar was John Michael Clarke MA of St John's College, Cambridge.

Horse-drawn bus travelling down Main Street, looking towards Leicester, *c.* 1905. The cottage in the centre background was Mrs Smalley's cottage; this has been demolished and now the Evington Library stands on the site.

High Street, *c.* 1920. The cottages in the left foreground have been demolished, and the post office now stands on the site. The thatched cottage at the end of the row has been retained and restored.

Cottages on Main Street, 1904. The Co-op store now occupies the site.

The same cottages, looking towards Leicester, *c.* 1920. St Denys Road now leads off to the right, and the cottage in the centre background is the Bridal Gallery.

Evington House, in use as an auxiliary hospital for wounded soldiers, 1918. Before the First World War it was the home of John Deardon. After hostilities ceased it was owned by Frank Howard Pochin, a manufacturer of inks and polishes.

Celebrating the coronation of George V, with John Edward Faire JP of Evington Hall addressing the gathering, 1911.

North Evington War Hospital, with stooks of corn in the foreground on land farmed by the architect Arthur Wakerley, 1918. Opened in 1905 as a poor law institution it became a hospital during the First World War and was named Leicester City General in 1930. In 1948 the word 'General' was dropped.

Shady Lane, laid out in 1850 by Sir Anthony Leigh-Keck of Stoughton Grange to provide some privacy to his rather exposed mansion, 1905.

The Glade on Hissops Lane, with Margery Steele walking towards Evington Hall, 1935.

Newhaven Road, formerly Hissop's Lane, 1979. This hedge could have been a thousand years old. It was removed in the name of progress shortly after this photograph was taken.

An engráving showing the church of St Denys standing in open fields, published in 1793.

Arboretum off Shady Lane, 21 May 1977. In this photograph Alexander Mackintosh is placing the ashes of his wife Eunice around the Pyrenean oak that they both sponsored when the arboretum was planted and laid out by Leicester City Council. On 20 March 1993 Alexander's ashes were placed on the same spot by his children.

Margery Steele and Alexander Mackintosh in front of the 'Old Cottage', Main Street (now no. 58), June 1937.

A.H. Soar's garage on High Street, 1938. This firm was the agent for Austin, Morris and Ford cars. Mrs Ruth Soar ran the local post office in the shop to the right of the doorway shown in this photograph.

Field footpath to Evington from Leicester from an oil painting by George S. Ramsay, 1910.

Samuel Hall sitting on his steam-driven road roller at Evington, 1928.

HUMBERSTONE

The Old Plough Inn when Joseph Cayless was landlord, 1904.

An engraving of St Mary's Church, viewed from the south, 1792.

Humberstone Hall, 1904. At this time Maurice Levy MP was the owner of this attractive house.

Playing bowls on the greens at Humberstone, *c.* 1920.

An aerial view of the village, showing the church of St Mary, top left, 1932. At that time the vicar was the Revd John Tarleton Hodgson BA of London University. Three years later Humberstone was transferred to the borough of Leicester under the County of Leicester review order.

The famous Humber Stone, 1910. Today only a small tip shows above ground, as it is slowly sinking into the subsoil. The stone, a large granite boulder, is believed to have been a Druid sacrificial altar. The most likely explanation for its appearance is that it arrived on the outskirts of Leicester as a result of volcanic action when the rocks of Charnwood Forest were being laid down, millions of years ago.

A Humberstone family, 1928. Back row, left to right: Charles Templar, Cyril Stevens. Middle row: Kate Clarke, Eva Templar, Nellie Templar, Betsy Stevens. Front row: Kate Templar.

A 4–6–0 class B1 no. 61188 passing through Humberstone station, pulling the 1.52 p.m. train from Mablethorpe to Leicester Belgrave Road station, 26 August 1962. This station was opened on 1 January 1883 and closed on 8 August 1962. Note the old Great Northern somersault signal, a survivor from 1883.

Humberstone Football Club, 1905. Back row, left to right: H. Smith, W. Templar (vice-captain), J. Knight, C. Towers, H. Bassett, A. Yorke, G. Templar, W. Payne. Middle row: W. Kenny, C. Wood, E. Wood, W. Bright, C. Fletcher (hon. sec.). Front row: J. Templar, R. Bright (captain), H. Yardley.

Two bricks manufactured at the Humberstone Patent Brick and Tile Company, Victoria Road. The manager in 1877 was Thomas Beech.

SCRAPTOFT

Scraptoft Hall, the residence of Capt. J. Burns-Hartopp JP, 1902.

The lake and gazebo in the grounds of Scraptoft Hall, 1904. The new resident was Alfred Cecil Grenfell.

Scraptoft Hall, by now the residence of Alfred Corah JP, 23 September 1920.

The Quorn Hunt on Covert Lane, Scraptoft, 1947. The hounds are being led by Major Cantrell Hubersty, and the whipper-in is Jack Littleworth. The boys walking alongside huntsman George Barker are Don Humberston and Terry Clarke.

Scraptoft Lane, 1927.

Ernest Jordan's carrier's cart at the junction of Scraptoft Lane and Uppingham Road, 1910. This carrier, based at Halstead, operated between Tilton-on-the-Hill and Leicester on Wednesdays and Saturdays. Left to right: Clara Jordan, Hilda Jordan, Ernest Jordan.

Early English stone cross in the churchyard with the vicarage in the background, *c.* 1902. This could be a market cross that was moved to its present position near the porch of All Saints' Church after it was blown down in 1895. The top of the column has been restored.

An engraving of All Saints' Church, Scraptoft, from a drawing by J. Pridden, published *c.* 1791.

38th Leicester Scout troop in camp at Scraptoft, 1932. Back row, left to right: Len Stanton, Bud Flude. Front row: Jack Roberts, Alan Moulden.

Laying water mains at Scraptoft, 1954. Gordon Moulden is looking into the cab of the contractor's excavator.

Peter Dawson clearing rubbish from the south-east corner of All Saints' churchyard during March 1989.

Cardinal Walk, off Scraptoft Lane, 1927.

T H U R M A S T O N

Melton Road, looking north towards Syston, *c.* 1910. The entrance to the Primitive Methodist Chapel built in 1884 is on the left (see page 35). The shop behind the horse and cart is now Hair Care, and Lea Close leads off to the right.

Melton Road, *c.* 1910. The house on the left is now Thurmaston Garden Centre. The cottages are Newark Villas and Pott Row, built in 1900. The shop at the end of the row is now J. R. Wine.

The Water Mill, Thurmaston. This photograph was taken a few years before the mill was demolished in the early 1930s; it is now the site of a boat-builder's yard. It was being run by Gibbins and Sons as a flour mill in 1925.

The weir and Johnson's Bridge (no. 17) on the Grand Union Canal, c. 1905. The arch on the bridge was removed in the 1950s and replaced with a concrete structure. The weir in the foreground has been rebuilt, and a footbridge now runs along the top of the brickwork.

Basin and boatyard on the Grand Union Canal. The water mill shown on page 31 stood on the site of this yard.

The narrowboat *Florence May* from J.R. & E.A. Blakes' boatyard, Thurmaston, moored on the Grand Union Canal.

In 1771 a Roman milestone was uncovered by workmen improving the road surface of the Fosse Way near the Thurmaston toll-gate. In 1783 it was incorporated into the column of the cross that stood in Belgrave Gate in the city of Leicester. This photograph is taken from the lithograph produced by John Flower in 1826. The cross was dismantled in 1844 and the milestone was then placed in the care of the Leicestershire Museums. It is now displayed in the Jewry Wall museum. The damaged inscription read:

IMP. CAES.
DIV. TRAIN. PARTH. F. DIV.
TRIN. HADRIAN. A. P. M. TR.
POT. IV. COS. III. A. RATIS
II

This has been translated as 'To the Emperor and Caesar the august Trajan Hadrian son of the divine Trajan surnamed Parthicus, grandson of the divine Nerva Pontifex Maximus; four times invested with Tribunitian power, thrice Consul. From *Ratae* [Leicester] two miles.' This stone, bearing a dedication to the Emperor Hadrian, records the fact that he was in his third consulship. He visited Britain and *Ratae* in AD 119 as part of his survey of Roman Britain. The upshot was that he gave instructions for the building of Hadrian's Wall in AD 122.

A brick manufactured at the Thurmaston Terra Metallic Brick and Tile Works, 1877. Thomas Barnard was manager at that time.

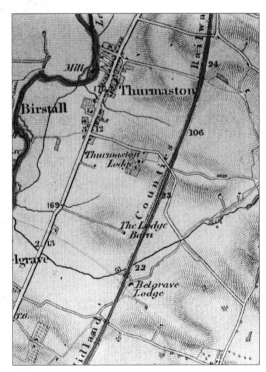

A section of the 1867 edition of the Ordnance Survey map featuring Thurmaston on the Fosse Way. Note the site of the water mill shown on page 31.

The church of St Michael, 1904. The Revd George Chappell was then vicar.

Building the Thurmaston bypass, viewed from Barkby Thorpe Lane, 1958.

An engraving of the Primitive Methodist Chapel, published during the year it was built, 1792. It was demolished in the nineteenth century, and a new building was erected on the site in 1884.

A gravel pit, Thurmaston. During the 1950s extensive gravel extraction took place to the west of Thurmaston, a far from modern process. In 1904 Clara Jane Austin was operating a sand and gravel business.

Canadian geese swimming in the nature reserve, Watermead Country Park, Thurmaston. It is hard to imagine that this idyllic scene was created from desolation such as that shown in the photograph above.

Walkers' crisp factory, which opened in 1948. This international company is at the forefront of modern advertising techniques. There can hardly be a household in the British Isles that has not heard of Walkers' crisps, manufactured in Thurmaston.

Potatoes being loaded into hoppers at Walkers' crisp factory, *c*. 1955.

Walkers crisps, the processing line, *c.* 1955.

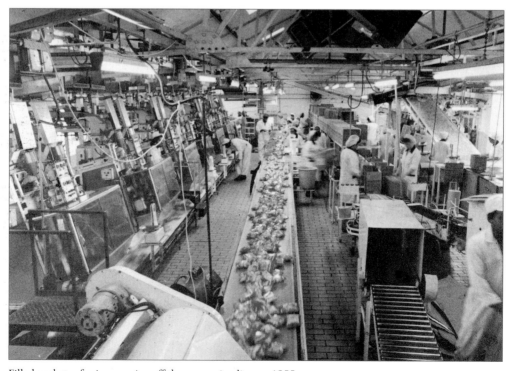

Filled packets of crisps coming off the processing line, *c.* 1955.

THURNBY & BUSHBY

The church of St Luke, Thurnby, 1904. The vicar then was the Revd Theodore John Redhead MA of St Edmund Hall, Oxford.

The Rose and Crown, Thurnby, *c.* 1950.

Thurnby Court in the year it was demolished, 1916.

The Fernie Hunt leaving Thurnby, 1938. Miss Hubbard's house is seen here; it has since been demolished and is now an open grass area.

The 38th Leicester Scout troop at Thurnby, Easter 1930. Left to right: Clifford Wright, Stan Wright, Arthur Shardlow, -?-, Alan Moulden, Roy Adams, Doug Taylor.

A 4–6–0 class B1 no. 61056 pulling the Leicester to Skegness excursion, passing through Thurnby and Scraptoft station on a wet summer day, 7 June 1954.

Thurnby and Scraptoft station, June 1954. It opened on 1 January 1883 and closed on 8 October 1962.

A 4–6–0 class B1 *Lord Burghley* no. 61247 enters Thurnby and Scraptoft station with the 1.20 p.m. Skegness to Leicester Belgrave Road train, 15 July 1961.

Thurnby Lane, Thurnby, *c.* 1905. The entrance to Holmleigh Gardens now leads off to the left, while the high building on the centre right has been completely rebuilt in a smaller matching style, and is now named Orchard House.

Minstrels who performed at the concert at St Luke's School, Thurnby Lodge, 1945. In the background is the Memorial Hall. Back row, left to right: John Cooper, John Compton, Alan Mountford, Colin Dishington, Don Humberston, Don White, Morris Letts. Front row: Roy Milner, Terry Clarke, Alan Britain, Geoff Elliott, Brian Robinson, John Holmes, Gordon Gulliver, 'Mr Interlocutor' Lesley Mills.

Thatched cottages that stood at the entrance to Bushby Hall, *c.* 1904. These were demolished in the early 1950s.

Main Street, Bushby, *c.* 1920. The photographer was standing in front of Randles Close; on the left no. 60, on the right no. 61.

SECTION TWO

EAST OF THE WREAK

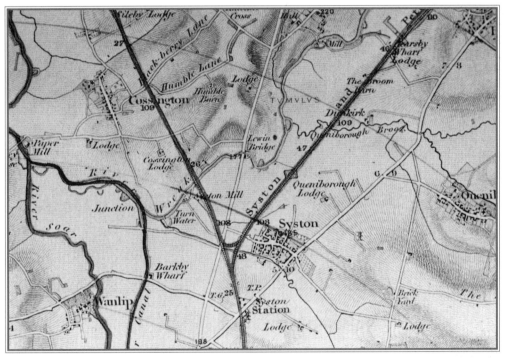

This section of the 1867 edition of the Ordnance Survey map shows Syston as a compact village. Queniborough was out in the fields. Syston railway station had been open for twenty-seven years with the windmill standing close by. A further windmill was situated out in the fields towards Queniborough.

BARKBY & HAMILTON

Main Street, Barkby, looking east, *c.* 1910. The post office and shop are near left, and the blacksmith's forge run by the Sharpless brothers centre left. Barkby Hall, the Pochin family home, is in the centre, while near right is the Malt Shovel inn (part of Merton College estate). The landlord was John Carnall. Note the gas lamps. Gas first came to the village in 1900 and was supplied to all the village in about 1940.

Barkby Hall, 1925. This was the home of George William Pochin DL, JP. To the right stands the church of St Mary, whose vicar was the Revd Llewelyn Wynn Watkin LTh of Durham University.

Main Street, Barkby, post office and shop, *c.* 1910. The village bakehouse was in the yard at the rear of this building. Mr Harry Hitchcox, proprietor and baker, is standing in the doorway with his daughter. His apprentice is holding the horse.

Main Street, Barkby, at the junction with Syston Lane, now known as Queniborough Lane, looking west, *c.* 1902. The small child standing in the doorway of the home of W. Illston, the tailor, is probably Katie Illston. A horse and cart are standing outside the Malt Shovel inn and the doors of the blacksmith's forge can be seen near right.

Dairy Farm, Barkby Holt Lane, Barkby, *c.* 1910. This formed part of the Pochin Estate and was farmed by the Kirk family for at least five generations.

Brookside, Barkby, *c.* 1900. Douglas Wyatt (with bowler hat), licensee of the Brookside inn, stands on the slate bridge with his family and friends.

Brookside, Barkby, *c.* 1906. A pair of mud and thatch cottages stand adjacent to the brook with two adults and a child standing on the plank bridge. These cottages were demolished in the early part of the century and a laundry house built on the site. Mrs Pawley took in laundry and Mr Pawley worked at Barkby Hall. A pair of semi-detached cottages (64 and 66 Brookside) now stand at the rear of the site.

Barkby United Cricket Club team, 1890. Back row, left to right: C. Cox, W. Kirk, G. Heggs, H. Kirk, G. Needham, umpire's name not known. Middle row: W. Sharpless, A. Sharpless, Alfred Kirk, H. Illston. Front row: J. Earl (scorer), D. Illston, Arthur Kirk. A feature of the matches between village cricket teams in this area was that a needle match always took place on a feast day. Barkby's feast was in the first week of September.

The Drive, Main Street, Barkby, *c.* 1912. Pheasant rearing. Here, near the game-keeper's cottage on the drive, the 'broody' hens are being pegged out for five to ten minutes to ensure they took food and water every day.

The wheelwrights' shop, Syston Lane, Barkby, late 1800s. The Sharpless brothers were wheelwrights and carpenters. The child holding the donkey is Sylvia Sharpless, whose father Frank and his brother were the village blacksmiths. They also travelled to smithies at Hungarton, Thorpe Satchville, South Croxton, Rearsby, Quenby Hall and Baggrave Hall.

An aerial photograph of the deserted hamlet of Hamilton, first recorded in the Leicestershire survey of 1130.

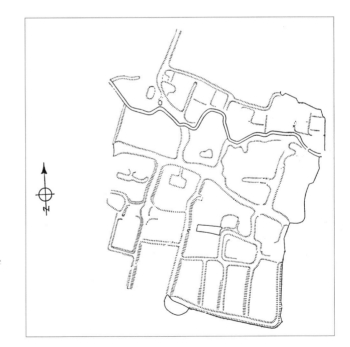

A plan of Hamilton drawn in the 1940s. Originally it was Hamela's village, a settlement that was part of Barkby. It was a deserted village by the 1450s almost certainly as a result of successive epidemics of bubonic plague during the preceding decades and later enclosure clearances.

Building the new village of Hamilton. Planning permission was given in December 1987 to build approximately 4,000 homes on 1,500 acres of land by the year 2006.

Developers working on a building site overlooking Barkby Thorpe. Houses are being built by Wimpey, David Wilson, J.S. Bloor, Westbury and Bellway, and a shared equity housing scheme is being developed by the De Montfort Housing Trust.

BARKBY THORPE

Milking time in the 'Bridge' field, Beeby Road, part of Manor Farm, Barkby Thorpe, 1904. At this time the farm was run by Richard Pick, who was also a market gardener.

Members of the Pick family in the stack yard at Manor Farm, *c.* 1910.

Fruit picking at Manor Farm, *c.* 1900.
Apples, pears, plums and damsons were
all grown for sale in the local markets.

A horse-drawn dray is loaded with 'bushel
baskets' of fruit ready for delivery to local
shops and to market, Manor Farm,
c. 1900. The building in the background
was formerly the site of a house; at the
time this photograph was taken it was
used as an apple store and a flower
bunching room for daffodils grown on
the farm.

BEEBY

The church of All Saints, 1895. The vicar was Revd Henry Cundy DD. Built in the Early English style, the octagonal spire was never completed. Local tradition has it that during the building operations the architects who designed the structure, two brothers, fell out over the method of construction and during the ensuing struggle fell from the battlements and were killed. The thatched cottage on the right of the photograph has been demolished.

North Leicestershire Brewery, constructed on the instructions of Thomas Nuttall in the late eighteenth century, situated on the Barkby Road, 1900. Built as the Beeby Brewery it was renamed the Midland Brewery at the time this photograph was taken. The manager was Job Facer.

The Quorn Hunt outside the Manor House, Beeby, 1890s. This was the main administration centre of the world-famous Stilton cheese maker, Thomas Nuttall. For further information consult *The History of Stilton Cheese*, 1995.

Thomas Nuttall opened the first factory for the commercial production of Stilton cheese in 1875. This radically altered the way this cheese was marketed. To meet the demand, Nuttall had to increase his milk supplies, extending his already large herd of dairy cows. In 1876 he built a row of farm workers' cottages off the Beeby to Hungarton road to house his farm workers, commemorating the venture with the date recorded in blue brick.

A village wedding at the church of All Saints, 7 April 1926. Back row, left to right: Arthur Fairbrother, William Davies, Sam Fairbrother. Front row: May Davies, Charlotte Fairbrother, Margaret Davies.

A Vauxhall car in the yard at Home Farm, 1931. Left to right: Sam Fairbrother, John Davies, Sarah Fairbrother.

Sawing logs for fuel in front of All Saints' Church, 1944. Left to right: Carmelo Louselo (an Italian PoW) George Newcombe, William Davies, John Davies.

A wartime shooting party, 1944. Left to right: William Davies, Carmelo Louselo holding a brace of pheasants and a hare. Sam Fairbrother holds the double-barrelled 12-bore.

Samuel Fairbrother was a village character who farmed out of Home Farm, a centre for Stilton cheese manufacture, during the interwar years. It was from this dairy that Charlotte Fairbrother produced some of her prize-winning Stiltons. Sam had a reputation as a serious consumer of home-made ale. This cartoon is extracted from a small book of cartoons that was produced to commemorate a famous victory by Barkby cricket team over Beeby in the 1930s, when Sam's ale drunk at the tea interval was the major contributory factor to why Beeby lost!

Samuel Fairbrother's personal barrel holding two quarts of home-made ale. Note his initials, S.F., branded on the oak bottom. When Sam was working on the farm, hay making, ploughing or following any other farming pursuit, this barrel of ale was always with him. He always consumed the contents before lunch and during the afternoon session he emptied the barrel again, consuming on average a gallon of ale per day.

QUENIBOROUGH

The village square, 1904. The Britannia inn is on the left, licensee John Tailby, and the Horse and Groom inn, licensee Charles Williams, is in the centre background. Standing in front of this building is a cyclist with a type of rickshaw in tow (see front cover).

Main Street, 1925. The church of St Mary with its prominent spire stands centre background. The vicar was Revd George Lowe Bennett MA of St John's College, Oxford.

Main Street, 1916. On the right is the Horse and Groom inn, licensee William Sansome. The village pump stands near the oak tree with the Britannia inn, where Mrs Ellen Tailby was licensee, in the background. On the left is Fox's tailor's shop.

The Methodist Chapel built in 1899 and opened in 1900, Queniborough Road, *c.* 1905.

Main Street, *c*. 1910. Note the 'gutters' at the side of the highway; these gained considerable notoriety because soap- suds mixed with blood from the local butcher's premises continually flowed down the channels.

The brick-built dovecot that now stands in a paddock near Queniborough Hall. Built in 1705 this structure was threatened by modern development and was moved to the present site, and rebuilt brick by brick in 1987, under a nationally funded preservation scheme.

The Old Hall, 1925. Possibly on the site of a medieval house, it was extensively altered and enlarged in 1672 by the Bennett family. It was the home of Capt. William Godfrey Higgins at the time of this photograph.

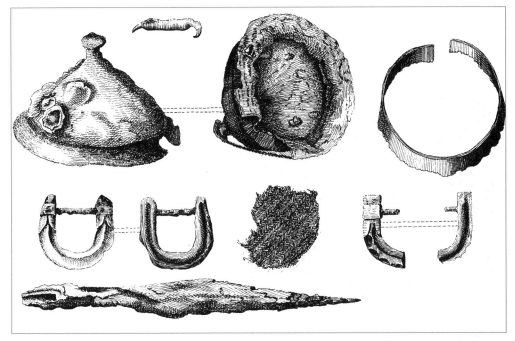

A selection of objects found with a Saxon burial at Queniborough. This was the grave of a chieftain or noble and was excavated during the late eighteenth century. The collection was placed in the care of Leicester Museums but is now lost.

SOUTH CROXTON

The Main Street, 1925. On the right is Harriet Leatherhead's shop. The church of St John, whose vicar was Revd Dudley Gibson Bishop MA of Pembroke College, Oxford, stands in the centre background.

South Croxton and District Home Guard, 1941. Standing, left to right: Lt Lea, S. Knap, W. Parker, C. Hall, J. Roberts, G. Naylor, -?-, J. Sarson, N. Fairbrother, J. Wilson, B. Kirk, B. Payne, G. Robertson of Sludge Hall. Among those kneeling: A. Fuller, R. Parker, F. Lee, R. Fuller, J. Payne, R. Muggleton, L. Knap.

Mrs Ann Draycott standing outside her cottage on Main Street, 1912. This house was the post office for a number of years until 1924. Demolished some years later, it was rebuilt and is now no. 48.

The tower of the church of St John the Baptist after being struck by lightning on 4 June 1936.

Inside St John the Baptist's Church, 5 June 1936. The vicar, Revd Frederick Clarke, and Lawrence and Les Knapp are viewing the damage caused when the lightning struck.

South Croxton Primary School, 1960. The headmistress was Miss Doves. Back row, left to right: Sally Ingram, Jane Pratt, John Elliott, David Ingram, Alan Adcock, Ann Haupt. Middle row: Lorna Adcock, Peter Townley, Gay Badbury, Neil Fairbrother, Jennifer Yates, Sally Sampey, Andrea Kent. Front row: Joy Badbury, Sheena Nicol, Peter Elliot, Philip Kent, Lesley Pratt, Marina Adcock, Rachael Wheeler.

Codswallop – A Pantomime, South Croxton village hall, 20 December 1980. Back row, left to right: Angela Crawford, Fiona Ginns, Naomi Aldis, Mark Crawford. Front row: Rowena Moss, Teresa Haupt.

SYSTON

High Street, looking towards the 'Flatten', *c.* 1900. The cottage on the right is featured on page 77.

School Street, *c.* 1900. At the end of the row of cottages the Primitive Methodist Chapel built in 1836 is just visible. All these thatched cottages were demolished during the 1950s.

The Fox and Hounds public house at the junction of High Street and Melton Road, 1907. At that time Percy Woodward Barradale was licensee. A granite horse trough stands in front of the entrance to the stables at the rear of the premises.

The war memorial that stood on the junction with High Street, Melton Road and Barkby Road, 1925. The Bakers Arms stands on the left, looking towards Leicester. This war memorial was erected in 1921 and removed and rebuilt in Central Park in 1972.

A motor vehicle accident at the war memorial junction, 1928. A steamer operated by Mountsorrel Granite Co. was in collision with two Model T Fords; all three vehicles had damaged front axles. In the two groups of onlookers stand 'Stubby' Burgess and 'Doctor' Garner, the local jobbing builder.

Syston Green, with the church of St Peter in the background, 1880. The vicar was Revd William Mitchell Croome MA.

Reg Cooper standing behind the counter in Cooper's off-licence on High Street, c. 1950.

Herbert Tilley's store, High Street, c. 1903. Left to right: Herbert Tilley jnr, Mary Tilley, Herbert Tilley snr.

Cooper's off-licence, corner of High Street and School Street, c. 1950.

Floods on the Fosse Way, Syston, during the winter of 1957–8.

Fowke's Garden Centre on the Fosse Way, 1984. This site is now a modern housing development.

Syston Boys' Brigade (11th Leicesters), 1959. The photograph was taken on the Memorial Playing Fields. Back row, left to right: Tom Coulson, Tony Carlisle, Stan Lockwood, Dave Read, Ray Young, Phil Sharp, Keith Yarwood, Pete Johnson, Ian Parsons, Terry Yarwood, Revd H. Holman, Bob Boswijk, Ted Court (captain). Middle row: Bob Spence, Robert Orme, Graham Lowe, Cedric Kirk, John Burton, John Orme, Robert Scott, Barry Hough, Lionel Sleath, Alan Graham, Gerald Cockrell. Front row: Jimmy Coulson, David Taylor, Robert Smith, Keith Stanyon, Kevin Garner, Alan Lowe, Geoff Kirk, John Lomas, Brian Yarwood, Howard Kemp, Stuart Reid, with the Leicester Battalion First Aid Shield won at the first attempt.

Syston railway station, when the station-master was Thomas Edward Bowers, 1904. In the background, left, are the stockyards for holding farm animals and produce. The traders shown are William James Iliffe, seedsman and florist, Whitaker the horsedealer and John Thomas Main, auctioneer and valuer. This station opened in May 1840 and closed in March 1968.

A 2–4–0 Kirtley no. 158a passing through Syston from Leicester en route to Saxby, *c.* 1920.

A 2–8–0 Stanier class 8F no. 8023 hauling a line of heavy goods wagons out to Melton Mowbray from Syston, March 1937.

Jackie Smith's cycle shop on Melton Road, opposite Goodes Lane, *c.* 1920. Jackie Smith is standing on crutches in front of his shop, next door to Aggars, stonemasons.

Cecil Ogden of St Elmo, Syston, 1902. This Leicester-based architect designed the Victorian estates on Spinney Hill (see page 9), Danes Hill, Humberstone and Belgrave, as well as the Granville Hotel and the first part of the Grand Hotel in Leicester.

Moody Bush Stone standing in a field off the Syston to South Croxton road. Legend has it that this is the site where the court of the Goscote Hundred was held on nearby Moody Bush Hill. Such courts were held in the open air on high ground wherever possible, to prevent interference from unwanted objectors.

The entrance to F. Payne & Son, Melton Road, *c.* 1925. This firm was a blacksmith and general farriers.

Coronation celebrations, planting silver birches by the footpath on the Memorial Playing Fields, 1953. Back row, left to right: Frank Payne, Harry Walker, George Heggs, Victor Pearce, Harold Gamble. Front row: Alan Oswin (with spade), Margaret Young, Ann Smith, and Harry Walker's dog, Ben.

Syston windmill when Edward Cooper was miller, *c.* 1905. This post-mill worked until 1908 and was blown down on 14 February 1910. Its trestle was unusual in that it had six quarter bars and three cross-trees instead of the normal four quarter bars and two cross-trees. The sails were 30 ft long and consisted of two common and two spring.

Syston windmill, the Midland Hotel and the entrance to the railway station goods yard, probably 1909.

A cottage on High Street being thatched by 'Big Bill' Sharp, 1930.

The same cottage after a disastrous fire in 1985. It is now the Cheeky Fox restaurant.

Syston Parochial Infant School, High Street, 1953. Mrs Browning's class, which took part in the Nativity Play in the old church hall, Broad Street, is seen here. Back row, left to right: -?-, -?-, Rosemary Harrison, Frances Tailby. Fourth row: -?-, Linda Winfield, Rosemary Bentley, Sylvia Palmer, Diane Swain. Third row: -?-, Sally Orchard, David Bottomley, Janette Payne, Pauline Pitcher, Janet Potter. Second row: Margaret Toon, Eunice Foster, Andrea Cox, Margaret Young. Front row: Margaret Black, Maureen Marriott, Carol Smith, Joan Clay.

Syston Operatic Society, 1958. This is the occasion of their second annual pantomime, *Mother Goose*, in the old church hall, Broad Street. Back row, left to right: John Tarry, Jennifer Hubbard, George Chapman, David Gaffney. Front row: John Buswell (Dame), Margaret Buswell, Betty Whalley, Christine Miller, Brenda Baker, Colin Wesson, Jessica Adcock, Frances Wesson, Sheila Helliwell, the little girl.

The Church Lads Brigade from the church of St Peter and St Paul being inspected, Empire Sunday, 23 May 1909. The vicar, Revd John Murch Tucker MA of Keble College, Oxford, rural dean of Goscote second area, is officiating.

Handbell ringers, *c.* 1880. Back row: J.W. Freeman, Revd W. M. Groome (vicar 1875–87), J. Pickard. Front row: G. Hitchcox, A. Carnell, B. Carnell, W. Rowe, E. Hitchcox, J. North.

Syston Conservative Club skittle team, 1920. Back row, left to right: Mr Cridland, J. Barradale, O. Widowson, G. Heggs, J. Moore, W. West, F. Gamble, J. Killingley, F. Payne, A. Payne, Alf Sharp. Front row: S. Ward, J. Adcock, T.R. Mansfield, H. Rowell, B.J. Gamble, A. Mansfield.

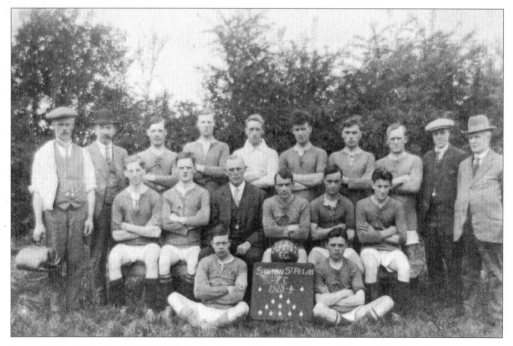

Syston St Peter's Football Club, 1923/4. Back row, left to right: David Lewin, Billy Wright, ? Kemp, Bert Smith, Ted Norwell, Pearce Cooper, -?-, Harold Smith, Clem Hawes. Middle row: Fred Hoares, -?-, Bob Marshall, Billy Foster, Andy Cooper, Reg North. Front row: Harold Lewin, Les Lewin.

IN THE GOSCOTE HUNDRED

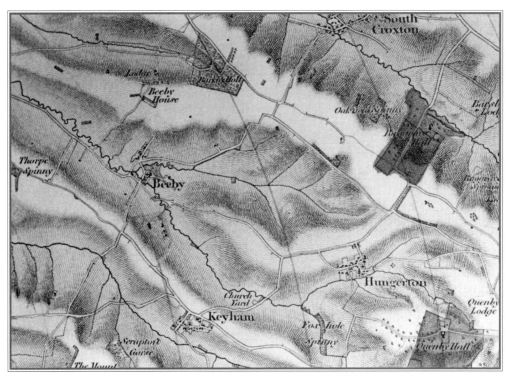

A section of the 1867 edition of the Ordnance Survey map showing the hamlet of Beeby, the village of South Croxton and Quenby Hall. These are points in an important triangle of agricultural land, possibly the birthplace of part of the modern cheese-making industry. The Ashbys farmed these lands in the sixteenth, seventeenth and eighteenth centuries as did Thomas Nuttall in the late nineteenth century, when he made Leicester and Stilton cheeses. A common feature mounted in paths and pavements to many houses in this area are bases of Leicester cheese presses made out of Swithland slate.

B A G G R A V E   H A L L

Baggrave Hall, the home of Algernon Edwyn Burnaby JP, 1910. There was a house near this site in 1352 when the Knights Templar were in possession of the estate. The present house was built in the middle of the sixteenth century by Francis Cave.

The meet of the Quorn Hunt at Baggrave Hall, 1985. This was a unique occasion because all three huntsmen, from the Quorn, Michael Farrin, the Fernie, Bruce Durno, and the Belvoir, Robin Jackson, were present.

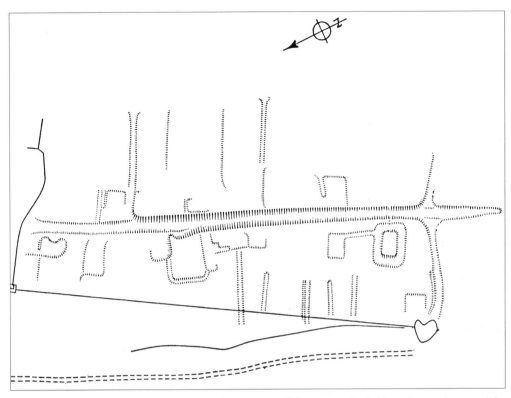

A plan of the deserted hamlet of Baggrave. This site can still be seen in the fields to the south-west of the present hall. The village is listed in the Domesday Book and would have had about sixteen households. The hall was then a fortified manor house. Depopulation took place as a result of park enclosures and house clearances commencing in 1500 when the Abbot of Leicester enclosed the lands, and by the 1570s all the families had been evicted.

Reconstruction of a Saxon wooden container uncovered in a burial mound at Baggrave in 1784.

HRH the Prince of Wales with Major
Algernon Edwyn Burnaby JP, MFH, at a meet
of the Quorn Hunt at Baggrave Hall, 1927.

Thimble Hall, which stood on the north-east ridge running along the edge of the Baggrave Estate, *c.* 1910.
This house with its castellated roof was built in the 1830s by Sir Frederick Gustavus Fowke, who was
made a baronet in 1814. He lived at nearby Lowesby Hall and erected this 'eye-catcher' to celebrate the
birth of his son and heir. It took fourteen days to build, fell into ruin in the 1970s and was pulled down. A
less romantic larger structure now occupies the site.

COLD NEWTON

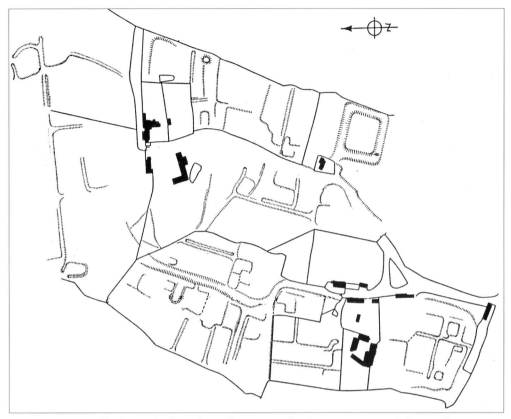

A plan of the partially deserted village that still contains a few houses. It is recorded as a village in 1086 and in the tax returns of 1377 there were possibly as many as fifteen occupied houses. The decline of the village came about again as a result of the enclosure awards that had been completed by 1641. Farmhouses were built out in the newly enclosed fields and the ancient houses were abandoned, without any decrease in the population of the area.

Tom Farmer in the fields of Cold Newton with Jim Holmes's shire foal, c. 1920.

Highfields Farm, built in about 1650 and seen here in 1973. Shortly after this a major restoration programme took place, when all the stucco was removed and the original stone was exposed.

Mr and Mrs Gamble outside their cottage at Cold Newton, c. 1950. This row of cottages was demolished shortly after the photograph was taken. 'Boy' Gamble was a poacher of some repute who roamed the fields and parkland around Cold Newton, taking game as he saw fit.

The crown equerry Sir John Miller and huntsman Michael Farrin leading the Quorn hounds at Cold Newton, 1986.

HRH Prince Charles with the Quorn Hunt at Cold Newton, 1984.

HUNGARTON

The church of St John the Baptist, when Revd John Ellis MA was vicar, 1910.

The posthouse, 1904. The sub-postmistress was Mrs Charlotte Wright. The building seen on the centre right is now Rose Cottage.

Godric House, now Jasmine Cottage, 1904. The wall on the right fronts on to the Wesleyan Chapel, built in 1845.

The elementary school was erected in 1875 at a cost of £300. This photograph was taken in 1904 when the headmistress was Miss Annie Hall.

Children standing on the main street in front of the blacksmith's forge, *c.* 1910.

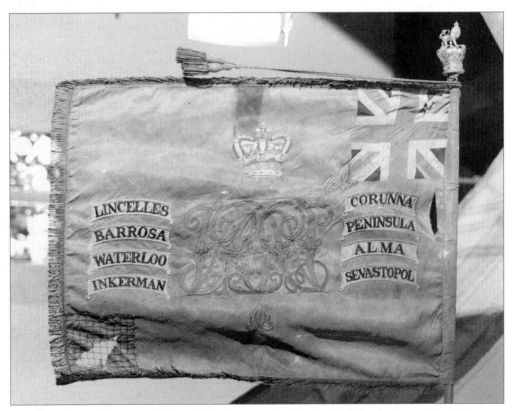

The military flag of the Grenadier Guards that hangs in the church of St John the Baptist. Battle honours: Lincelles, France, 1793; Barrosa, Spain, 1811; Waterloo, Belgium, 1815; Inkerman, Crimea, 1854; Corunna, Spain, 1809; Peninsula, Spain, 1811; Alma, Crimea, 1854; Sevastopol, Crimea, 1855.

South view of the church of St John the Baptist, 1925. The vicar at the time was Revd Cecil Lloyd Matthews.

The Ashby Arms public house (licensee Job Flint) viewed from the church porch, 1925.

Geoffrey Hayward, David and Eric Barnett standing in the snow with the Black Boy public house in the background, during the severe winter of 1947.

Excruciating cold work! Cutting kale at Sycamore Farm, Hungarton, in winter 1947. Left to right: Robert Barnett, Thomas Farmer, -?-.

David, Robert and Eric Barnett at Sycamore Farm, 1948.

Hungarton Women's Institute, 1949. Back row, left to right: Connie Bates, Mrs Brewster, Mrs Macdowel, Mrs Nelson Gamble, Mrs Thornley, Mrs Keene (president), Mrs Inder, Mrs Bates, Mrs Preston, Mrs Riley, Mrs Spark. Front row: Marjorie Howe and her son, Violet Apperley, Mrs Thorpe, Mrs Apperley, Ethel Cole, Mrs Brewster's daughter, Mrs Barnett, Mrs Warrington, Mrs Wattam, Mrs Edgar Bates, Mrs Chapman, Miss F. Gamble, Mrs Payne.

KEYHAM

A panoramic view of Keyham, 1904. In the centre background stands the church of All Saints, whose vicar was Revd Richard Burton MA of Lincoln College, Oxford.

The County Council School built in 1885 at a cost of £420, seen here in 1904. The headmistress was Miss Rosetta George.

Keyham viewed from Wood Lane (now Covert Lane), 6 June 1952.

The Old Hall, the home of John Cross, 1905.

Harrison's Foundry, 1921. Robert, Rowles, Cissie, Mavis and Ethelwyne Harrison are posing in a large pump liner casting made in their father's foundry.

Clarrie Timson at work in the Harrison foundry, *c.* 1930. For further reading consult *A Foundry in a Garden* by Rowles Harrison (Sutton Publishing,1995).

The post office and village shop, *c.* 1914. This small business closed down in 1972 having been run by Miss Gertrude Healey for over sixty years.

Quorn huntsman Michael Farrin on Isle of Man with the Quorn hounds at the Hungarton, Ingarsby and Beeby Road junction, Keyham, 1982. The dilapidated barns in the background have now been converted into a modern bungalow.

38th Leicester scout troop at a weekend camp at Keyham, June 1934.

A 'rough and tumble' at the weekend camp of 38th Leicester scout troop, June 1934. Left to right: Wag Rhodes, -?-, George Pollontine.

QUENBY HALL

The west front of Quenby Hall, drawn by Frances Flora Palmer and published on 1 September 1842. This artist was born in Leicester in June 1812, the daughter of Robert and Elizabeth Bond. She married Edmund Palmer in 1832. With her husband she emigrated to the United States of America and by the 1850s had established herself as one of the leading printmakers in New York. 'Fanny' Palmer is regarded as one of the most important lithographic artists of her era in the United States.

Quenby Hall was built on the instructions of George Ashby between 1615 and 1620. It is a magnificent Jacobean house constructed from brick, considered by many people the finest house of its type and period in England. The Ashby family started enclosing the parkland in the late 1400s, absorbing the open fields into hedged units to hold cows for milk and meat production. Quenby gained a reputation for fine cheese production, producing a unique cheese in the late seventeenth century named Lady Beaumont's cheese, later to be known as Quenby cheese. This was a lightly pressed cheese, yellow in colour. Blue veins appeared under the crust when it was fully mature. Today it would be considered a cross between Red Leicester and Blue Stilton, and may have had a similar taste. The farm dairies around the Quenby estate eventually developed the manufacture of Stilton and Red Leicester as two separate cheeses. Relics of the early days of cheese production can still be found at the many scattered farmhouses in the area and also at Quenby Hall. The bases of Leicester cheese presses cut out of slate and granite are used as decorative flagstones and in some instances doorsteps.

From about 1715 Quenby Hall fell into disrepair and the Ashbys became absentee landlords for over forty years. In 1759 the hall was sold by Warring Ashby to his cousin Shuckburgh Ashby who restored the hall and outbuildings, and built up the estate into a prosperous farming community. The estate gained a national reputation for its production of Stilton cheese. From the late eighteenth century up to the present time it suffered at the hands of various owners. It has been well restored by the present owner, Squire de Lisle, and can again be considered one of the finest stately homes of its type in England.

Front view of Quenby Hall, when the owner was Sir Harold Stansmore Nutting Bt, 1925.

Quenby Hall, 1925.

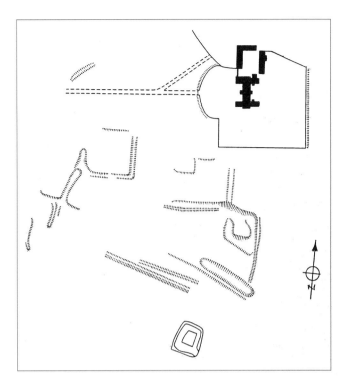

A plan of the deserted hamlet of Quenby with the present hall shown at the north-east corner and what appears to be a moated manor house on the south part of the site. It is more likely to have been a partially filled-in fish pond. Quenby derives from the Old English name, cwene-burg (the queen's manor), and may have formed part of an Anglo-Saxon queen's endowment. In the tax return of 1377 there were between eight and ten houses on the site, all to be swept away during the Ashby family's park enclosures, instigated between the years 1485 and 1489.

Western Avenue leading to the hall, during the occupancy of Alfred Russell Donisthorpe, 1904.

Quenby Hall, viewed through the entrance to Ingarsby Lodge Farmhouse. This farm produced excellent Stilton cheese from the 1880s until 1961.

The sunken garden when it was maintained by Sir Harold Nutting, 1925.

Quenby hounds at the entrance to the garden, 1905.

The cottage in the park, *c.* 1920. This was demolished in 1980.

'The Monk's Rest' cricket pavilion that stood in the park, 1926.

Quenby Lodge, in the park to the north-east of the hall, 1973. The lodge was built in 1775 by Shuckburgh Ashby as an 'eye-catcher'.

Edric Nutting on Duster, and John Nutting on Game Cock, 1925.

The night nursery at Quenby Hall, 1925.

Lady Nutting, John Nutting, Sir Harold Nutting, Edric Nutting, Anthony Nutting, 1925.

Princess Ingrid of Sweden on French Maid in Quenby Hall stableyard, 1926.

HH Princess Helena Victoria of Schleswig-Holstein, grandchild of Queen Victoria, near the summer-house in the sunken garden at Quenby Hall, 1926.

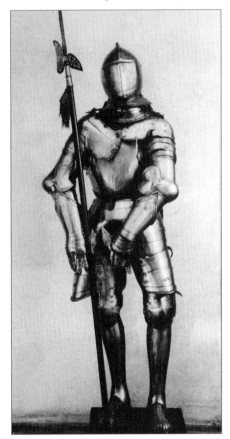

English Civil War armour of about 1640, Quenby Hall.

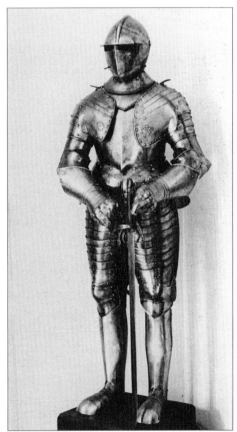

Germanic armour of *c.* 1550, Quenby Hall.

Fancy dress, July 1926. In this group standing in the courtyard in front of the steps to the east wing of the hall are: Rupert Hardy, Lady Nutting, Anthony Nutting, Princess Helena Victoria, Edric Nutting and Princess Ingrid of Sweden.

Anthony Nutting on Babette in the stableyard at Quenby Hall, 1927. Anthony eventually became the MP for the Melton and Rutland division and is famous in the history of this country for his decision to resign his seat in the House of Commons over the Suez Crisis in the 1950s.

The ballroom, Quenby Hall, during the occupancy of Lady Henry Grosvenor, 1910.

The ballroom, Quenby Hall, during the occupancy of Sir Harold Nutting, 1925.

The princess bedroom, 1925.

The angel bedroom, 1910.

The angel bedroom, 1925.

The library, 1925.

The library, 1978.

The front hall, December 1973.

The front hall, 1977.

The pomegranate room, 1977.

The kitchen, 1925.

The kitchen, November 1978.

The restoration of the Hall in full progress, shortly after it was purchased by the present owner, Squire de Lisle, 22 July 1974.

The clock tower, January 1974.

Michael Farrin and the Quorn hounds leaving Quenby Hall, *c*. 1985.

Squire de Lisle and his son Peter greet the passengers in the horse and trap at the bridle-way turn in front of Quenby Hall. Wendy Holliday is the driver.

OUT TO THE
TILTON RIDGE

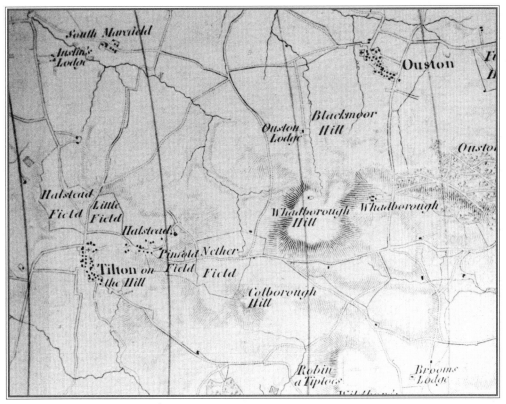

A section of the 1867 edition of the Ordnance Survey map. Tilton-on-the-Hill sits on top of Marlstone Ridge, a tract of iron ore-bearing rock that was extensively mined from open-cast pits sunk at Halstead. These pits became a focal point for geologists because of the Jurassic deposits that were uncovered as the mining progressed.

HALSTEAD

The Oakham road, Halstead, 1936. The spire of the church of St Peter, Tilton-on-the-Hill, is visible in the centre background. Revd Harry Victor Floyd AKCL was vicar at this time.

Tilton railway station, Halstead, 5 December 1953. This is the view from a carriage window as the last 1.44 p.m. Northampton to Melton Mowbray train leaves the station. This station opened on 15 December 1879 and closed on 7 December 1953.

Tilton railway station, Halstead, 5 December 1953. An 0–6–0 class 4F, the last 10.47 a.m. Nottingham to Northampton train, is just leaving the station.

Tilton railway station, Halstead, 5 December 1953. The last 2.30 p.m. Market Harborough to Melton Mowbray train is just arriving, double-headed by a Webb 1890 design LNWR 'IP' 2–4–2T, followed by a British Rail class 4 MT.

Mr and Mrs J. Hall outside their cottage at
Halstead, 1940.

Mr and Mrs Goodman, known to all the villagers as 'Mammy and Billy', sitting outside their thatched
cottage Glenbower, 1928. This cottage was demolished. A modern house was built on the site and given
the same name.

Jack Randell and Horace Lawrence hand picking iron-ore for loading into wagons at the Tilton (Halstead pit) open-cast ironstone mine, 1928.

Open-cast ironstone mine, Tilton, 1928. The engine-driver is David Ferguson. Back row, left to right: Arthur Downs, -?-, Joe Scattergood. Front row: Fred Warrington, Jack Farr, James Randell, -?-, -?-, -?-, -?-, -?-, -?-, -?-, -?-, Harry Stapleford in the trilby hat.

Ironstone miners and an 0–6–0 Bagnall tank engine at Halstead pit, 1934. In the cab are David Ferguson (left) and Tom Eaton; standing on the track is Jack Burnett. The pit was opened in 1880 and closed in 1961.

The Salisbury Arms public house, c. 1905. John Otter was then licensee, and the Otter family is seen here posing outside the main entrance.

The old Salisbury Arms closed its doors for a number of years from 1983. This photograph was taken in the tap room on the last night. Left to right: Bill Woods, Eddie Scales, Rodney Vickers, Joan Scales (landlady), Graham Voss, Ruth Vickers, Terry Vickers.

The Salisbury Arms was purchased by Geoff and Anita Pike in 1985. Here Thorndike building contractors are seen refurbishing the building.

HOUGHTON-ON-THE-HILL & INGARSBY

The church of St Catherine stands proudly in the centre of this aerial view, 1960s.

Ray Lockley, butcher's boy from Aldwinckles, delivering meat on the A47 on his BSA, *c.* 1945. George Davis is in the horse-drawn cart, and the Rose and Crown public house and Sunny Brae garage are on the left.

Main Street, *c.* 1935. On the left is Church Farm; on the right stands the magnificent line of elm trees planted in 1640. They were cut down because they became unsafe 320 years later.

The Poplars, Main Street, 1936. Next to it is the Black Horse public house (licensee John King); on the right is the entrance to the Methodist Chapel which was built in 1852.

Snowdrifts at Houghton-on-the-Hill, March 1917. Left to right: John Dixon, Violet Dixon (later Mrs Orton), Henry Dixon in the pram; pushing the pram, Dorothy Dixon.

The same group on the same occasion; Houghton-on-the-Hill on the A47, looking south.

Main Street, 1920. Work had just commenced on laying out the site of the village hall. Without permission, a gap was cut in the hedge on the left which allowed George Squire's cows to wander down the highway, causing some damage in the village.

Houghton-on-the-Hill windmill, 1905. It ceased grinding corn in 1894; the last man to work it was Alfred Gray. An unusual feature was the hand-wheel at the back of the cap that was used for turning the sails into the wind. The mill was sold in 1920; it was then demolished and a house was built on the site.

The First World War memorial standing on the junction with Main Street and Scotland Lane, erected in 1921. The four halves of two stones from the windmill were set in the grass verge. They are just visible in this 1930s photograph. These stones are still positioned next to the base of the memorial. Unlike most village memorials, this monument does not record any service personnel killed in the Second World War, as everyone who served returned safely.

A picnic in a cornfield off Stretton Lane at Home Farm, *c.* 1945. In the centre are May and George Davis.

Empire Day, 1923. This is the Church of England primary school; on the extreme left stands Mr Herrick, a local farmer who ran the gardening class. All the children are well equipped with the necessary gardening tools. Back row, left to right: William Blackwell, Eddie Garfoot, Jack Radford, Lionel Radford, Naomi Orton, Dorothy Orton, Catherine Harris, Rene Fielding, Physie Davis, Miss Radford. Front row: Maurice Squire, -?-, -?-, -?-, -?-, Jack Holmes, Dick Fielding, Ernest Cochrane.

A country dancing group at the garden party held in the rectory grounds, 1923.

Sunday school outing, *c.* 1925. The wagonette, with a party of pupils en route to a picnic on Borrough Hills, is driven by William Davis.

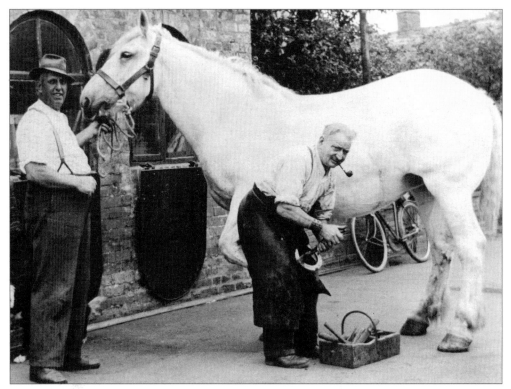

Replacing a shoe at the blacksmith's shop, Main Street, *c.* 1960. Left to right: George Davis, Kate the horse, Charles Partridge, the village blacksmith.

A convoy of ash tree trunks being conveyed down Main Street on horse-drawn wagons, *c*.1930.

The morning after a German bombing raid on the village, 15 March 1941. Furniture is being removed from damaged cottages that stood next to the blacksmith's shop. These cottages were later demolished and the rectory was built on the site. Houghton-on-the-Hill suffered from three bombing raids during the Second World War.

Outside the pig sty at Home Farm, *c.* 1935. Left to right: George Davis, Elsie Davis and Sam the pig.

Houghton-on-the-Hill Cricket Club, winners of the Market Harborough Golden Wonder Cup, 1979. Back row, left to right: Golden Wonder representative Tom Smart (chairman), Mark Hanford, John Ford snr, John Ford jnr, Peter Oakes, John Elliott, Jim Funnell, Arthur Bambury (umpire), Ian Abbott (president). Front row: John Boulter, Chris Brown, Mort Stephenson (captain), Ian Maxfield, Miss Maxfield (scorer), Peter Burgess.

'Chappie' Harris and Peter Harris shearing sheep and wrapping wool at New Ingarsby Farm, 1952.

In the hay field at New Ingarsby Farm, summer 1954. Back row, left to right: Betty Harris, Pauline Harris, -?-. Front row: Peter Harris, Bill Glennon, Jim Clay.

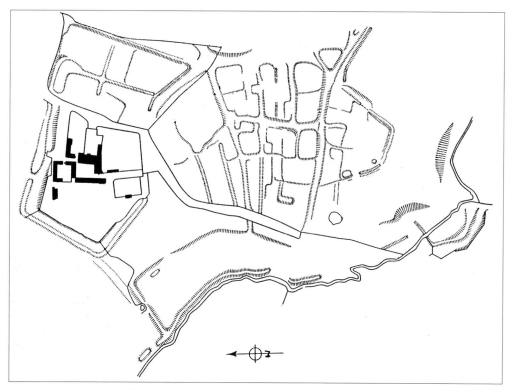

A plan of the deserted village of Ingarsby. The name means 'Ingwar's village', Ingwar being an ancient Danish personal name. It is recorded in the Domesday Book as having a population of thirty-two. There is evidence that it suffered from repeated outbreaks of bubonic plague; in the tax return of 1334 its quota was one of the lowest in the country. In 1469 it was 'cleared' by Leicester Abbey, which enclosed the whole area for sheep and cattle grazing.

The Quorn Hunt at Ingarsby, 1983. Left to right: Sir John Miller, Harry Kesselring (groom at Quenby Hall), HRH Prince Charles, Barbara Rich and James Teacher (joint masters), Squire de Lisle, Mrs Ronald Brookes.

Mrs Orton standing in the doorway of High-Leys Farmhouse, 1903. This farmhouse stands in the fields off Covert Lane, south of Scraptoft, and is now a ruin.

The 11.20 a.m. Leicester to Skegness train passing through Ingarsby and Houghton railway station, 2 August 1954.

Ingarsby railway station, 1904. Opened on 1 January 1883 as Ingersby on the Great Northern line, in September 1939 it became part of the London North-Eastern system as Ingarsby. It closed on 8 October 1962.

Ingarsby railway station, late 1940s. The passenger service for this station ceased on 7 December 1953.

LOWESBY

Lowesby Hall, the home of Sir Frederick Thomas Fowke Bt, DL, JP, 1891.

Sir Frederick Ferrars Conant Fowke, 3rd Baronet of Lowesby Hall, 1902. A lieutenant in the Leicestershire Imperial Yeomanry, he saw action in the Boer War.

In 1834 Henry de la Poer Beresford, 3rd Marquis of Waterford, took a lease on Lowesby Hall for three years. In December 1835 for a wager of one hundred guineas he jumped a five-bar gate placed next to the fully laden dinner table, in front of his astonished guests. His exploits were legendary; he was the leader of the gang who 'painted the town red'. See page 33 of *Melton Mowbray in Old Photographs*, 1993.

Nicholas Nuttall and Lady Nuttall in front of Lowesby Hall, 1940.

Clarence Jordan and Mrs G.H. Kirkpatrick leaving the stable yard at Lowesby Hall, 1947.

Clarence Jordan driving the tractor with Arthur Bonshor, Bill Frith and Adrian Jordan in the wagon, *c*. 1950. Lily Jordan is holding her daughter Rosemary and John Sparks, head gardener of Lowesby Hall, is leaning on the fence.

The Leadbetter family harvesting wheat at Lowesby Grange with a Titan tractor pulling the binder, 1925.

The Leadbetter family thrashing corn at Lowesby Grange, c. 1925.

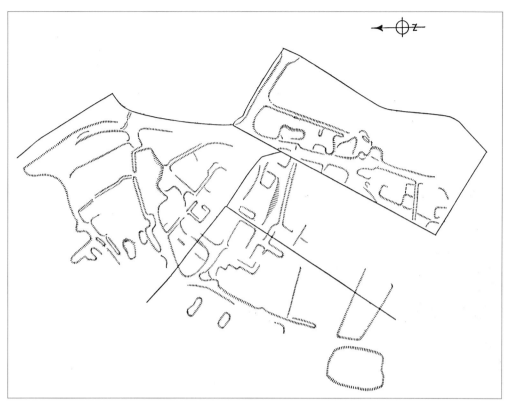

The deserted village of Lowesby was probably founded by the Danes in the late 800s. In 1086 there could have been as many as nineteen houses in the village. A steady decline in the population took place and it was probably affected by the Black Death. It was enclosed in 1487 by the Ashbys, who cleared the land and immediately converted it for sheep and cattle grazing, as was their custom. Unlike many deserted medieval villages, the church has survived.

Gwen Jordan on a hay rake at Caudle Farm, 1926.

Gwen Jordan at Caudle Farm with dray and stacking elevator, 1942.

A Titan tractor drives an elevator in 'Big Seeds' field near Lowesby Grange; a worker is stacking hay, *c*. 1930. The photographer was Bill Leadbetter.

George Middleton cutting grass for hay making at Lowesby Grange, 1930.

Church of England school, Lowesby, 1951. The school opened in June 1876, most of the cost being met by Sir Frederick Fowke. Back row, left to right: Kathleen Vickers, John Voss, -?-, Pearl Ward. Front row: Norman Farmer, Michael Stapleford.

Church of England school, Lowesby, 1921. Left to right: Gwen Jordan, Gladys Leadbetter, Alice Richardson.

Lowesby railway station cottages, 1944. Left to right: Doris Hockney, Gerald and Jennifer Butler.

Loseby railway station, 1916. This station opened on 1 January 1883 as part of the Great Northern system. It was renamed Lowesby in December 1916, when the station master was Harry Horton. It closed to passenger traffic on 29 April 1957 and finally closed to all traffic on 8 October 1962.

Railway gangers servicing the track at Lowesby station, 1920. In this group are Bill Goodman, Ernest Jordan, Fred Holmes and Tommy Bryan.

Joseph Mutch looking out of the north signal box at Marefield Junction, 1962. The Saturday only northbound freight from Leicester is just passing.

A 0–6–0 Class J39 entering Lowesby station, 1953.

Passengers who have just left the last 1 p.m. Leicester to Melton Mowbray train at Lowesby station, 15 December 1953. Left to right: Alf Baines (porter/signalman), Joan Clarke, Margery Mutch, Gwen Mutch, Doris Leadbetter, Vera Smith.

The north signal box, Lowesby, June 1958.

MAREFIELD

May Leadbetter and Elizabeth Leadbetter outside Snows Farm, Marefield, 1900. A few years later the tenant farmers living at this house were the Oliver family. Arthur Potter Oliver gained a considerable reputation as a fine Stilton cheese maker (see page 99 of *A History of Stilton Cheese*, 1995).

Florrie Wilford and Bill Wilford in a farm cart being pulled by Snowy at Marefield, 1943.

Cutting wheat at Marefield, August 1945. Left to right: Elsie Wilford, Archie Crawford, Reg Kettle.

Marefield west signal box, *c.* 1920.

T I L T O N - O N - T H E - H I L L

Main Street, looking north, 1910. On the right stands Brookside House. The road to the left is Back Lane and that to the right is Loddington Road. The church of St Peter stands high in the background.

Loddington Road, 1938. On the right stands Ashdene; on the left are Bank Cottages; in the centre stands a row of three cottages that have now been converted into one house.

A pony and trap in the yard of the Rose and Crown public house, 1908. The landlord was John Hall. Left to right: Mary Jane Hall with the twins Frank and Sam Hall.

The wheelwright's shop, 1907. On the left Jack Pepper and Dick Griffen are standing in the doorway; on the right is the blacksmith's shop with Jim Randell and Tom Payne standing outside.

The church of St Peter, 1904. The vicar was Revd William Chippindall MA of Trinity College, Cambridge.

Pony and trap on The Bank above the Loddington Road in front of Woodbine Cottage, 1905.

Charlie Handley's bus from Tilton-on-the-Hill, 'A day out at the seaside, 1930'. In this group are Fanny Vickers from the Salisbury Arms, Halstead, Mrs Hopwell, George Vickers, Major Furlong and two grooms from Laund Abbey.

A rabbit-shooting and digging party at Tilton-on-the-Hill organized by John Otter of the Salisbury Arms public house, Halstead, 1912.

A group of children standing on The Bank opposite Tom Orton's outdoor beerhouse on Loddington Road, 1930. Left to right: Jack Bird, Elsie Wilford, Edie Randell, Connie Downs, Win Scattergood.

The stile on the footpath from Lowesby railway station to Tilton-on-the-Hill, 1934. Left to right: Clara Jordan, Hilda Baines, Alf Baines, Cyril ?, Neville Baines.

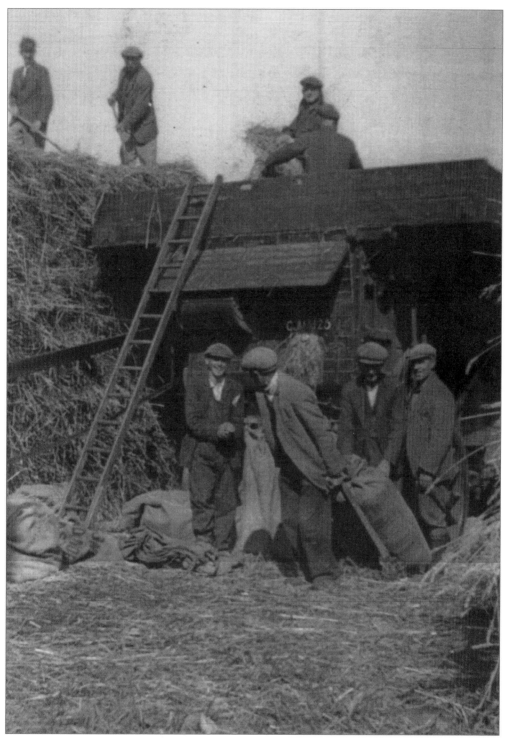

Threshing wheat at Manor Farm, 1943. On the stack and threshing drum, left to right: Michael Carpenter, Tom Orton, Sergeant Glover, -?-. In front of the threshing drum, left to right: Bill Voss, Albert Farnsworth, Oliver Strickland, -?-.

Walter Knapp and Joe Voss shearing sheep at Springfield Farm, 1950.

Throughout the 1950s and '60s one of the great weekend attractions was the Tilton-on-the-Hill motor-cycle scrambling meet. It was patronized by cyclists throughout the Midlands and beyond. John Voss is in action on a BSA on the hillside course at Springfield Farm, 1965.

Garden fête, 1927. Back row, left to right: Flo Turville, Betty Bradley, May Downes, Kitt Randell. Front row: Aggie Knapp, Phyllis Payne, Joan Vickers. Below: children taking part in the celebrations to commemorate Queen Elizabeth II's Silver Jubilee, 7 June 1977.

		Adam Rymer		Andrew Lockyer		Tracey Palmer		
Darren Malatesta	Roger Smith	Lisa Palmer	Jonathan Lawrence	-?-		Fiona Smith	Simon Whitmore	Michaela Keeling
	Robert Blandon	-?-		Richard Whitmore	Sean Gill	Amanda Snowden	Lynne Mason	Mandy Darrell
	Russell Blakey	James Mason	Paul Lawrence	Cameron Hickling	Jamie Meakin	Karen Casson	Angela Malatesta	

-?-

Tilton-on-the-Hill windmill, *c.* 1910. The man in the doorway is the miller William Large. It is fairly certain that this mill was moved to this exposed site in the 1830s, from a less prominent position in the village.

The post-mill looking north, *c.* 1910. It was positioned on a good site 710 ft above sea level on the edge of a north- facing escarpment, well exposed to the north-easterly winds.

ACKNOWLEDGEMENTS

The photographs used in this book come from a variety of sources, some from the author's own personal collection. Very many were obtained through the efforts of the author's brother-in-law, Michael Mason, who lives at Tilton-on-the-Hill and knows the district well having worked in the area for many years. He contacted many friends, who then helped the author prepare this collection. Squire de Lisle allowed the author access to his amazing collection of photographs and many have been reproduced. The author's grateful thanks are also recorded to: Edith Parker, Edna Bird, Alan Moulden, Gwen Mutch, William Diebanck, Alan Cooke, Nigel Moon, Rowles Harrison, Robert Barnett, Sylvia Barnett, Pam Voss, Aggie Vickers, George Vickers, Prof. E Davis, Elsie Gunfield, Barbara Hall, Elizabeth Harris, Mr & Mrs Terry Toms, Don & Jo Humberston, Alan Stevens, Ray Young, John & Victoria Davies, Ray Davis, Alan Wright, Elizabeth Hornsby, Geoff Pike, Edward Gamble, Julian Duxbury, Gorden Williams, Nick Rooney, Pete Johnson of Walkers' Snack Foods.

Many of the photographs are out of copyright, but where copyright has been retained, permission has been granted to publish. Should this not be the case, the author offers his sincere apologies and will make an acknowledgement in a future edition. Finally, thanks are due to Morag Clarke for processing the manuscript for the publisher's use.

The author and the artist Rigby Graham discussing a local history publication outside The Black Boy inn, Hungerton, summer 1983.

LIST OF PLACES

Tilton-on-the-Hill windmill, looking south, *c.* 1910.